D1602514

This is

*permission*

Written by M.H. Clark
Designed by Justine Edge

This is *permission.*

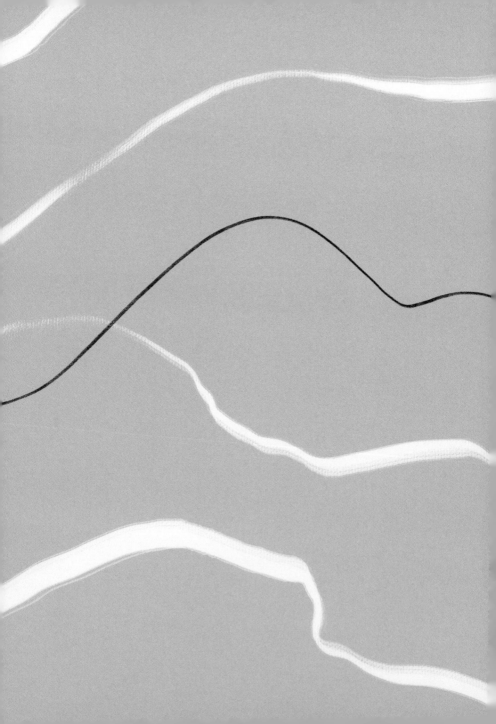

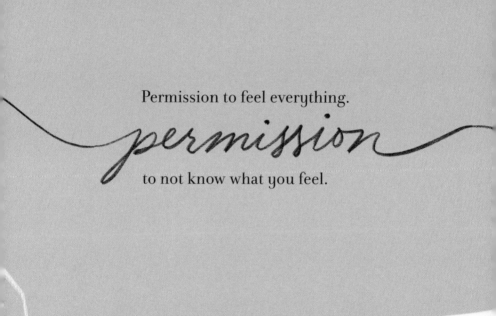

Permission to feel everything.

*permission*

to not know what you feel.

This is

*permission*

to contradict yourself.

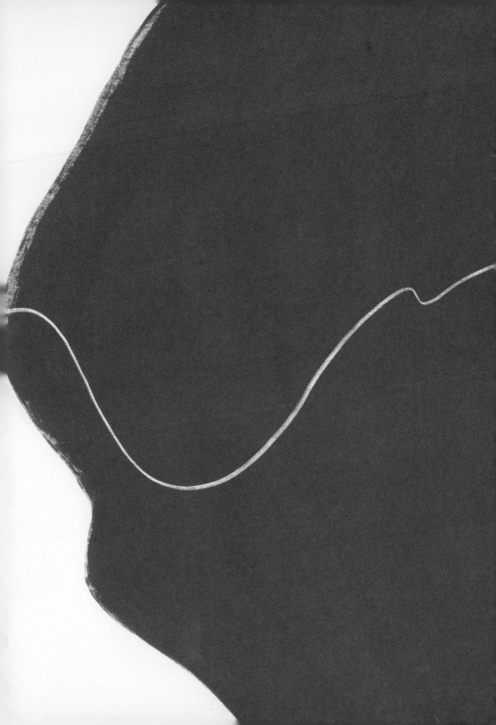

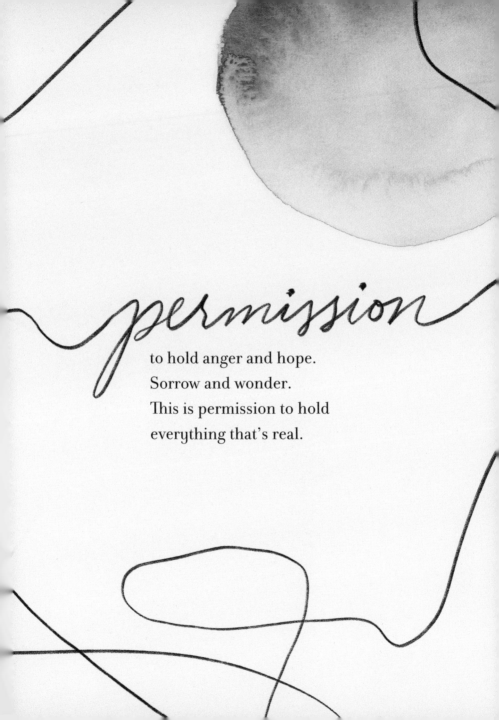

*permission*

to hold anger and hope.
Sorrow and wonder.
This is permission to hold
everything that's real.

You are allowed

to be a different person today
than the person you were yesterday.
You are allowed to change.

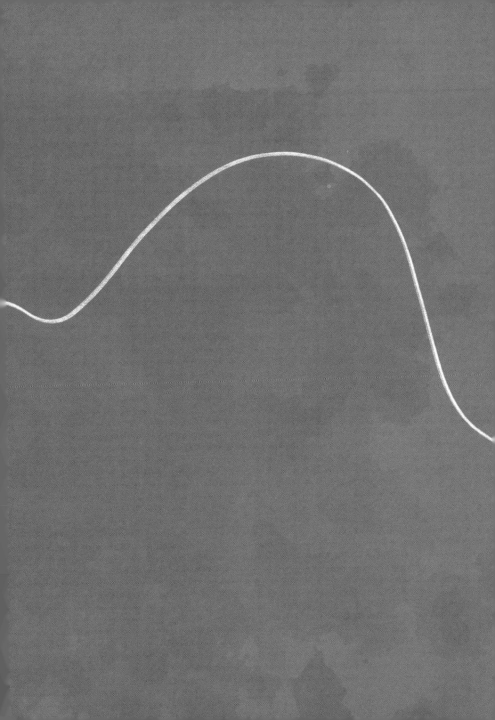

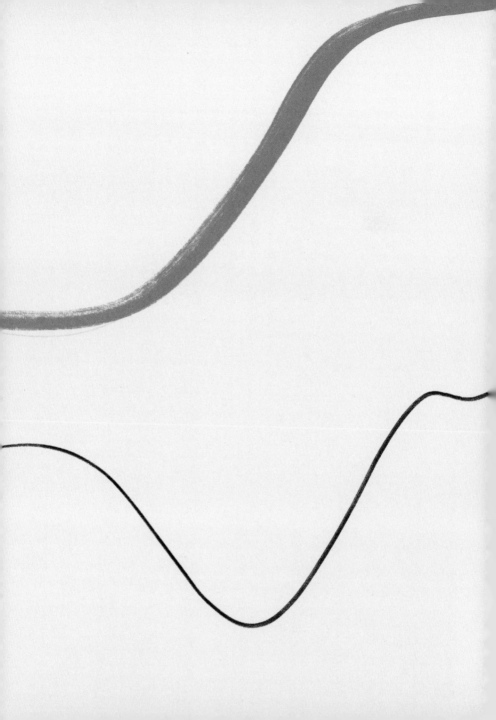

You are *allowed*
to mourn.
And you are allowed to need.

To look forward. To look back.
To be here, in this place.
And to grieve, if you need to grieve.

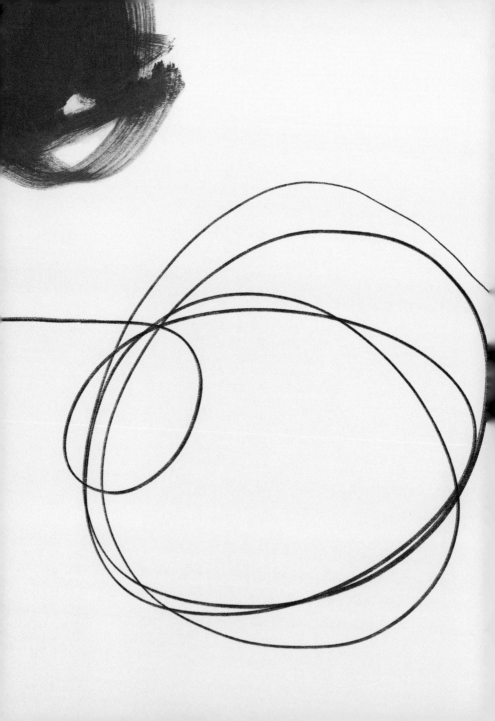

This is
_permission_

to make a mess.

Permission to be honest.

Permission to say what is true.

It is *alright* to ask to be seen, and to ask to be listened to.

It is *alright* to be here with your body,
to offer it attention,
to hold it with great care.

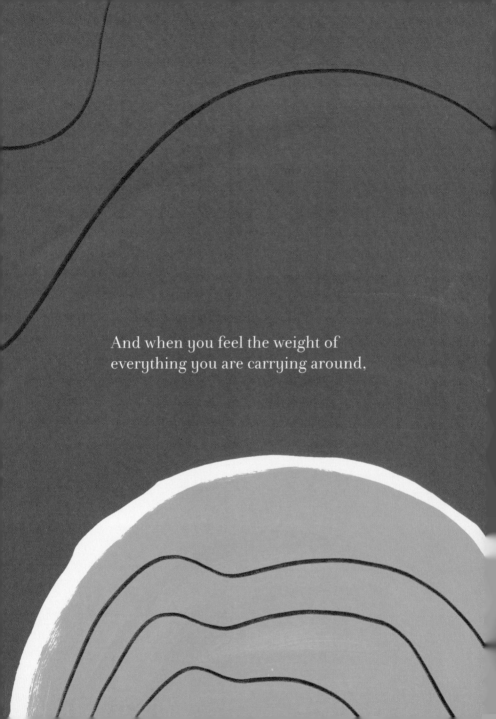

And when you feel the weight of
everything you are carrying around,

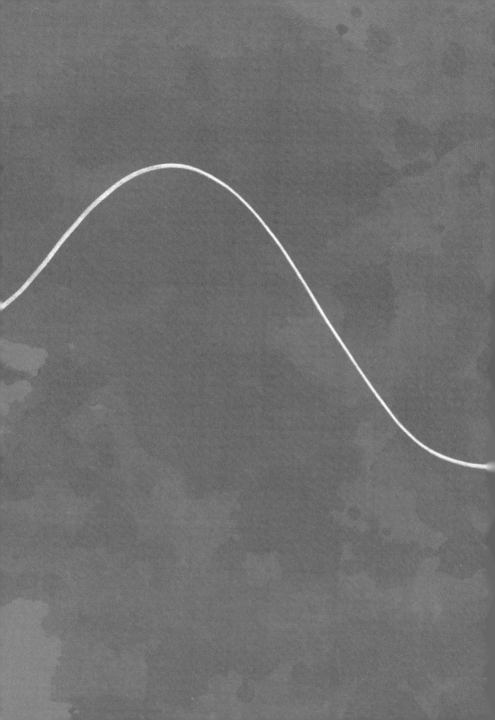

...it is

*alright*

to be tired.
Alright to rest.

*alright*

to let some things go.
To set some things down.

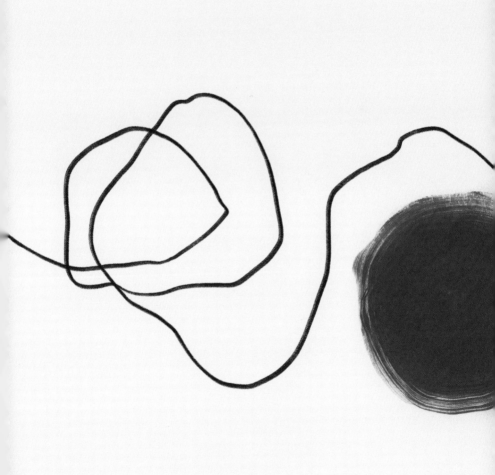

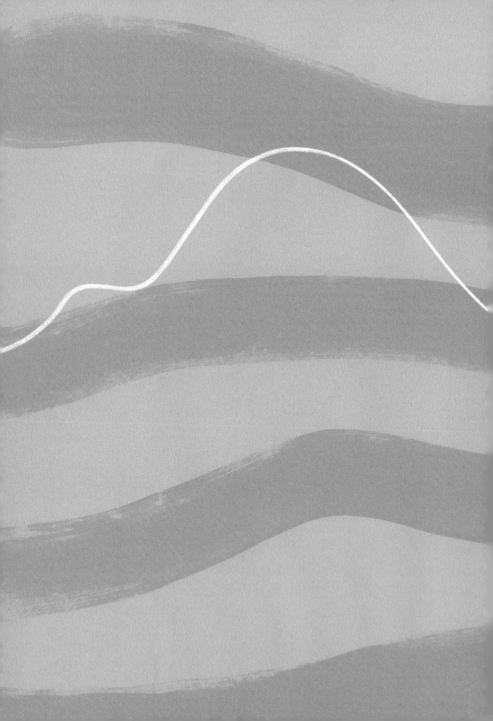

This is

*permission*

to know what you know.
To want what you want.
To need what you need.

It is

*alright*

to not apologize.

It is

*alright*

to speak
about what hurts.

It is *alright*

to tend to yourself.
To offer yourself gentleness.
To care for yourself first.

This is

*permission*

to not want this.
Permission to rage.
Permission to fight.

This is *permission*

to reach for whatever feels healing.

*permission*

to acknowledge the light.

You are

*allowed*

to let the feelings arrive.
Truth after truth,
moment after moment,
day after day.

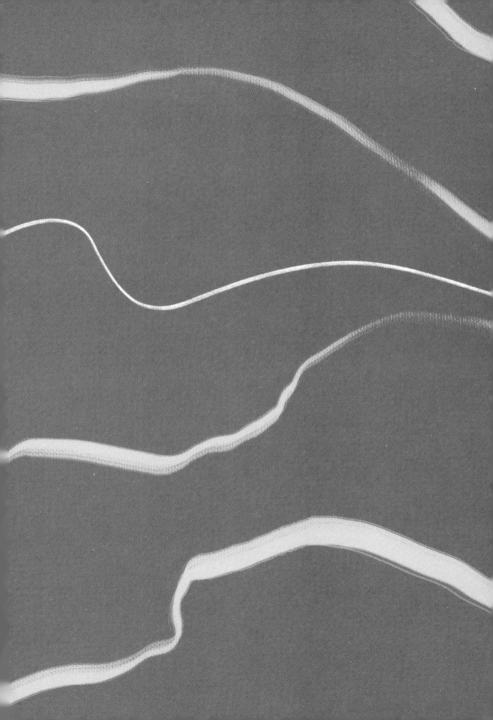

You are

allowed

to not be okay.

And to keep on anyway.

You are *allowed*

to remember you are as whole
and as huge and as real
as you have always been.

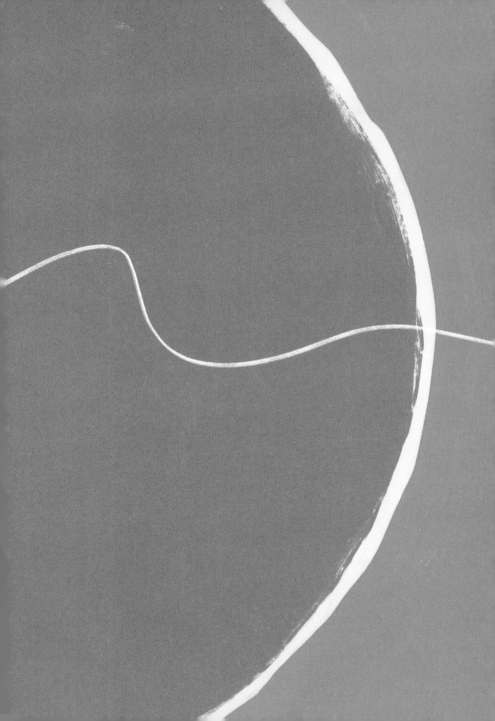

And to remind yourself
of this as often as you need.
Over and over, again and again.

This is

*permission*

to acknowledge what is here.
And to know that no matter how big it is,
you are still even bigger than this.

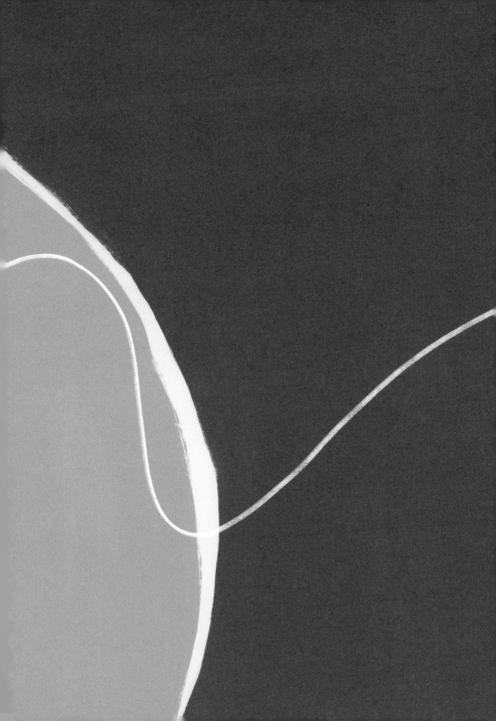

This is

*permission*

to think about tomorrow.
And to let tomorrow bring you
gently toward it.

COMPENDIUM.
live inspired

Written by: M.H. Clark
Designed by: Justine Edge
Edited by: Cindy Wetterlund

Library of Congress Control Number: 2019948218 │ ISBN: 978-1-970147-01-8

1st printing. Printed in China with soy inks on FSC®-Mix certified paper.

*Create
meaningful
moments
with gifts
that inspire.*

CONNECT WITH US
live-inspired.com │ sayhello@compendiuminc.com

    @compendiumliveinspired
#compendiumliveinspired